C000165798

Making A Few Quid/Bucks

Author

Stephen A Smith

A guide on how to make money in your spare time

Copyright

Introduction

At some time during our lives, there have been times when we could all have done with some extra money. Being short of money can be quite a stressful and worrying time for an individual and their family members. Not knowing where the next meal is coming from or how to pay the bills can lead to stressful situations, family rows and breakdowns in relationships. There are many instances where we all overspend more than we have budgeted for, or used credit cards, taken out loans, even borrowed off a friend without giving a thought to how we will repay our debt. Maybe you have borrowed money to buy presents for a family celebration such as birthdays or Christmas or even borrowed money to go on that long-awaited holiday.

When reading this book I am going to help you discover the secrets of making extra cash. Secret is perhaps the incorrect word. It's not really a secret; it is more like using your common sense and putting ideas into practice. Throughout my book I will make suggestions and guide you through proven ways of "making a few quid" (Bucks) $$$/£££

This is not a get rich quick scheme and it will not make you rich overnight. You will need to devote your spare time and effort. You will have to develop your plan, set your goals, make costings and in some cases, learn a few new skills.

There are many ways to make money some are easy, and others are more complex and require careful planning and development of new skills. You need to be dedicated and be in control. Most importantly, you should never ever give up.

How many people ignore their debt hoping things will get better and they never do. How many people in debt are frightened to answer their front door? How many people sit at home hoping something will turn up? How many people just lie in bed or laze around the house and watch TV hoping the debt will go away? Do you want to be one of those individuals or do you want to break free?

Please read my book thoroughly and follow my ideas, suggestions and guidelines on "making a few quid." (Bucks) You will be surprised how a little bit of time and effort can result in a wonderful income you never would have dreamed of, and in a few weeks, you will see the results of your efforts. Also, if your partner, family and children can lend a helping hand and devote some of their time towards helping you achieve your goals, it is even possible to double or treble your rewards. Are you the person who looks at an idea that someone else has dreamed up and gone on to become a millionaire? Have you asked to yourself, why didn't I think of that idea? Well if your answer is 'Yes' then join the rest of us! To be realistic the likelihood of you coming up with a multi-million-pound creation like the Microwave oven, the Rubik cube, or the Dyson vacuum cleaner are quite remote. You may be lucky! You never know! However, for now let us stick to making real money. Money, you can touch, save or spend!

Table of Contents

Idea number twenty

Idea number twenty-one

Idea number twenty-two

Idea number twenty-three

A Few Tips

My book shows you how to make money you would otherwise never have had and how to use your spare time and creativity to enable you to develop new skills. The secret is, discovering a service or product which is in public demand or by creating that demand for your own product or service. Next, you must discover a product or service to meet that demand. Set out a business plan, which is very important, especially to set goals and track your progress. You will need to source your product, craft your product by hand or create your service (Supply and demand is the key) Advertising and customer satisfaction are two key elements to attract new business and keeping customer loyalty.

Ask yourself, how much time and effort does it take to make ten pounds, ten dollars or ten Euro in an hour. The answer is not much time at all, it is quite easy. All you have to do is decide which idea in this book you are going to follow, make a plan and then it's all down to you. You will need to be enthusiastic, strong willed, self-motivated and have a belief and confidence in your product and yourself to succeed.

Ten pounds, ten dollars or ten Euro doesn't sound like a massive amount of money, however just by sacrificing one hour per day or one day per week and producing a net profit of £10/$10 per hour will earn you £70/$70 per week, that's £280/$280 per month by one individual. Supposing two members of your family each produce the same profit, you can expect to have a total extra monthly income of £560/$560. Not bad for a little time and effort!

Once you have chosen an idea you will need to set out a business plan. This is not a difficult task as you are writing down a story of what and how you would like your venture to realistically develop in the future. Your business won't necessarily follow the expectations you set out in your business plan. You must choose an idea from this book which suits your skill level and learning capacity. Using the skills and strengths you already possess gives you a head start and will help you on the road to success.

To be successful you need to be confident and believe in what you are doing. Bear in mind that materials and advertising can be achieved at a low cost and sometimes can be free. Working from home or considering running a mobile business, can be the best way of keeping overhead costs to a minimum and at the same time maximising your profits.

Sourcing and costing materials & setting your hourly rate for services

- Calculate overhead expenses
- Calculate transport and mailing costs
- Post & Packaging
- Advertising
- Outlet or customer
- On time-Right Price-Quality-Reliability & Delivery

The next step is to keep an inventory of materials and services including costs, gross profit, and net profit, hourly rate x time. Do your homework, source various outlets and look for ways to sell your products or services. Remember: Find or create a Demand = Fill the demand with a Product or service = be competitive set a fair price = Customer care = loyalty and repeat custom…Ask for feedback and recommendation.

So, let's get started, your first task is to choose a product or service which you can sell to customers/clients. Your product can be sourced from hundreds of suppliers on the internet, Trader magazine; The World's fair/market trader, professional wholesale suppliers and cash and carry's. Products such as watches, jewellery, cosmetics, or the latest gadgets or children's craze can be sourced on the internet or from the magazines I have mentioned.

Other products can range from arts and crafts, home-made jams and other preserves, costume jewellery, 'T' Shirts, mugs etc.

Another example of 'making a few quid' is to become an agent earning commission from a mail order supplier. For example: Avon cosmetics, Better Ware. Working as an agent has its drawbacks and will result in your profit margin being reduced considerably. The supplier takes the lion's share of the profit. My advice would be to do your own sourcing and buying, set your own profit margins and work from home to maximise profits.

Services are slightly different, in that you do not have to produce a product or purchase stock. Services range from Cleaning, Caring, Valeting, Sewing, Gardening etc. Some require a certain amount of skill such as sewing. However, others require very little skill at all. Remember it is your choice as to which idea you decide to follow. Therefore, it is important to measure your skills and competency against your choice of service or product you decide to sell.

Outlets and customers

Outlets or point of sales in some instances can be through the internet by setting up an account with online market places such as E-Bay, Google shop, Facebook, Fiverr and ESTY. You can also sell door to door or by booking a table at craft & trade fairs, car boot sales, Garage sales and markets etc. Other outlets could be country fairs, shows, parades and processions. It is all a question of choosing the right product for the right venue. For instance, if your chosen venue is held in the evening, such as firework displays, lantern processions, annual illuminations and Christmas light switch on ceremonies. The perfect product to sell would be light up gadgets. These are available through world fair magazine and internet suppliers. Usually you will be able to negotiate a discount for bulk buying.

If you were to choose horticulture as your business, the ideal outlet to target would be flower shows, county fairs, markets, agricultural shows and even car boot sales.

It is all down to common sense really! Choosing the right product and service to match the venue is the key to

success. For example, selling what is popular in the summer e.g. ice cream,
Beachwear or sunglasses and switch to selling hot dogs and burgers, scarfs and gloves in the winter. As they say, 'it's not rocket science.'

The most difficult thing is turning your idea into reality, by getting out there and doing it! Not just thinking about it!

Idea number one

Cleaning is my number one idea to make extra cash in your spare time. Cleaning can be carried out by most people without a great deal of skill or training and requires very little outlay to get started. There are hundreds of professional people who work full time and cannot find time to clean their homes or business property. There are also hundreds of old and disabled people who are unable to do their own cleaning. These are all potential customers, who are looking for a trustworthy person who will carry out their cleaning duties on a regular basis.

The most important part of doing home cleaning is 'Trust'

Other important things to consider are insurance cover for breakages and to agree with the customer what exactly they require from you e.g. do they require Vacuuming and dusting of all rooms. Or do they require cleaning of bathrooms and kitchens.

It is always a good idea to agree to the tasks being performed. Then draw up a contract with them so that there are no disagreements later. If extra work is required, then this can be agreed and added to the contract later, at a desired date.

Now you need to agree whether or not the customer supplies the cleaning tools and detergents and the hourly rate you are to charge for your services.

Bearing in mind at the time of writing this book the minimum wage is currently £7.20p in the UK and the UK government has pledged to raise it to £9.00. In the USA the average minimum wage is around $11.50 per hour. Therefore, it would not be unreasonable to charge a customer £12 per hour in the UK and $16 per hour in the USA.

So, assuming you decided to charge £12 per hour UK and $16 per hour USA excluding cleaning products and detergents. You spend one day per week and visit 3 clients spending 2 hours cleaning, your days labour would produce £72 UK and $96 USA. Monthly = £288 UK and $384. Not a bad return for 6 hours work!

You have now decided to spend some of your spare time to 'make a few Quid/bucks and you have decided to start by creating a 'cleaning business.' Q. What now? A., you must find your regular customers! Q. How do you achieve this? A. By advertising! Firstly, think of a good name which promotes your business as being special.

Example:

- Supreme Cleaners,

- Spick and span

- Home Valeting Services.

Now you need to sell your services. This can be done by various means and at very little cost.

<u>Example</u>

- leafleting door to door
- Face book
- Supermarket advertisement displays
- Approach local businesses such as estate agents
- Local Shops, Restaurants, and offices

Print a poster using your computer or have someone create one for you. Target your local disability associations, social housing associations and residential homes. Post leaflets around your area or if you own a car you could place a poster in the windows of your vehicle. Or take advantage of the advertising space in local shops.

You are all set to roll out your part time business. The phone rings and you have your first line of enquiry. Keep calm, and be polite and professional. Have a desk aid handy by your phone setting out your sales pitch and an appointment book beside you.

The desk aid will help you remember what to say and your script will make sure you don't miss anything out when talking to your customers. Explain what you do and what you charge, explain your signed contract agreement which covers workmanship guarantees and insurance cover for damages. Mention you are a member of a professional cleaning association and you can supply references and referrals if required. Sell your business with positive words such as a friendly, caring, honest and trustworthy.

The next step is to arrange a visit to your client's home. Enter the informal appointment in your diary. When visiting your client make sure you are punctual, smart but casually dressed, be polite, show your identity and ask them to call you by your first name. Let your client explain what they would like you to do and arrange with them how to gain access to their home or business and how to secure their property afterwards. Agree a day and time of the week when you will carry out your services. Sign and date the contract with them and give them your calling card or key ring contact information and their copy of the contract.

Assure your client of your professional, friendly and reliable service.

You must now ensure your cleaning ability is second to none. You must deliver your services on time and to a good quality standard and at the agreed price. You will find in the coming months that your client base will grow and providing you keep to a high standard your clients will stay with you and will recommend you to others. A word of warning, do not be blasé about your work or cut corners. If you have a slap dash attitude you will fail.

"Keep your standards high to succeed."

There are several variations of cleaning other than home interiors e.g. Window cleaning, exterior house plastics cleaning and carpet and upholstery cleaning. The same principles need to be observed as in home and office cleaning. Window cleaning can produce £10 per house and carpet cleaning you can expect £2 per square metre 6m x 4m carpet £42 plus detergent. 2 carpets per day =

£84 profit = £336 per month. Your carpet cleaning or window cleaning venture will entail some extra cost. You may have to hire a carpet cleaning machine or possibly a ladder. Alternatively, you may be able to borrow this equipment from friends to get started.

Idea number two

There is a lucrative market in sewing, although certain skills are required, and the ownership of a good sewing machine is vital. If you already have these skills you are half way there. If not, then you may have to ask a friend for help or enrol for course lessons at your local collage. There are many products you can make and sell.

Example:

- Kitchen pinafores
- Children's clothes
- Shopping bags
- Pet toys and bedding

Material supplies can be obtained from internet suppliers or you could browse the many charity shops to source cheap materials by re-cycling clothing, curtains and bedding.

Many people hoard old bedding and curtains and sometimes it is worth asking friends and neighbours if they have any old material items they would donate or sell to you for a small price. Jumble sales, car boot sales and garage sales will sometimes contain reusable materials and are worth visiting. Once you have obtained a pattern or sketched and made templates of the products you have decided on making, you would be well advised to practice making them. When you are satisfied with your creative products, the time has now arrived to make a display of your unique products and take good photographs of them.

Now is the time to test the market and hopefully sell your products and deliver a great profit.

There are several ways to market your products, such as Amazon, ESTY, Facebook, Google, and E-Bay or even consider starting your own website to promote your products. Craft fairs, markets and country fairs and shows can be useful venues to sell products.

Example: assuming you decide to start making home-made pets toys, for instance stuffed mice for cat's playtime. By using recycled clothing material salvaged from your local charity shop. With some imagination and inspiration, you should be able to produce ten small pet toys in an hour and providing they are unique and well displayed they could well fetch a retail price of £2.99 ($3) and that would equate to £30 ($30) for an hour's work. For instance, attaching the toy to a printed display card created with the help of a PC or packaging them in a colourful and appealing way will make your product look professional.

There are many other areas where sewing can be utilised to produce a good income.

Example:

- Making alterations to clothing
- Designing and making curtains & cushions
- Rag dolls
- Bags & hats
- Fancy dress

However, you must be determined to succeed, and you must develop your skills and develop new products.

A success story

I can recall a lady who discovered a product by accident. She was dusting around her home and couldn't remove the dust from underneath her television and gas fire. The dust had collected there for quite some time. She took a plastic twelve-inch rule and wrapped her duster around it, using it as a makeshift tool to remove the dust. Later that day, she visited her local plastics supplier and purchased a fifteen-foot piece of plastic trim, the same dimensions as the rule. She also bought some fluffy material used to make soft toys, some card material and a box of polythene bags. That evening she cut the plastic into sixteen-inch lengths and also cut the fluffy material into strips twelve inches long.

The lady then commenced sewing the material inside out, leaving an opening at one end; she then took hold of the pieces of plastic and pushed the now tubular material to form the fluffy side out. The open end of the material was then glued to the plastic and the remaining four inches of plastic was shaped into a handle. The card was later cut to the required shape and design printed. The dusting tool she had made was slipped into the polythene bag and the nicely printed card was folded in half and stapled to the bag. I heard that she then sent samples to various companies and eventually she received an order for fifty thousand items and repeat orders followed. Her profit was £1 per item. She has paid off the mortgage on her house, acquired a new car and has a secured savings in her bank account.

Idea number three

An interesting hobby and pass time is metal sculpture, which can easily be turned into a very lucrative business. All you need is a shed or garage to use as a workshop, several tools such as safety wear, a bench, a Mig welder, a grinder, a selection of files, tin snips, Blow torch and various bending tools. Jigs can be self-made as required. Very little skill is needed apart from practicing your welding skills. This idea of making money is more suited to the creative person who doesn't mind getting dirty.

To begin I will introduce you to some very simple sculptured items and I will give you tips and guidance on where to source your materials. Some materials can be found in your garage or sourced from your local scrap yard or rubbish dump.

What you need to bear in mind is; other people's rubbish can be turned into someone else's treasure. A good source for inspiration is the internet and in particular 'You tube' where you can source lots of interesting ideas and instructions on how to design, manufacture and apply a good finish to your metal artwork.

Example of easily obtained materials

- Nuts, bolts, nails and screws
- Old bicycle frames and parts
- Old hinges
- Cutlery

The materials listed can be used to create small sculptured items such as quirky figures and display items such as cars, motorcycles, animals, and figurines. Using a few pieces of scrap metal and a bit of imagination anyone can create unique sculptures at very little cost.

Using your tools i.e. your blow torch and pliers/mole grips and vice you can shape steel to your required design and then use your welding equipment to assemble and fabricate your sculptures. These can be painted or for a really professional finish they can be nickel plated. These small sculptures will retail for £20 and produce a handsome profit. These can be sold using e-bay, craft fairs, ESTY, Facebook or by supplying local shops.

As you become more experienced and gain competence in designing, fabricating and welding, you can expand your catalogue of products. You can focus on personal items for seasonal events and celebrations such as Christmas, Birthdays, Valentines and wedding gifts.

Another interesting product is metal wall art and garden sculptures. These have become very popular in recent years. Tin sheet metal can be purchased from a supplier, or alternatively scrap car body material can be used, although this gauge of sheet material is harder to work with. However, it is a cheap alterative to purchasing new material. Old tin cans, biscuit and sweet tins can be used however a fine welding wire or oxy acetylene gas welding is preferable.

If you become really ambitious you could easily produce hanging baskets, wall brackets, gates and railings, although this requires some skill in measuring and obtaining fairness of form = true, square and plumb.

First and foremost, you must consider your health & safety making sure you have good ventilation in your workshop and your tools are in good working order. You should acquire and wear safety goggles, leather gauntlets, welding screen with a No 12 filter or reactive lenses and a good quality overalls, preferably fire proof. Ensure electric cables are neatly stored and free from damage and move them away from welding, grinding and hot materials. Always have a water trough handy for cooling materials and a fire extinguisher as a precaution.

Idea number four

Costume Jewellery is my next suggested venture. There are several ways to start, either by making your own unique designed products such as rings, necklaces, bracelets, bangles and broaches by following instructions in jewellery making. You could however purchase ready-made jewellery at wholesale prices for re-sale. There are lots of ideas designs and tutorials available and it can often be fun for the whole family. Your products can be manufactured in your own home on those cold dark winter nights.

A success story

A friend of mine tours the flea markets and care boot sales purchasing solid silver Victorian tea spoons. He then cuts off the scoop end and remodels the spoons stem around a steel bar to form an adjustable solid silver ring complete with silver assay mark and beautiful Victorian hilt design. An average priced silver spoon costing £5-£10/$5-$10. The rings retail for £80/$80. The left-over scoops of the spoons are melted down made into silver ingot necklaces, which also retail for £80/$80

Another method is to purchase your ready-made jewellery from a supplier on line or from magazines such as The Trader. Items can range from watches, leather wrist bands, gold plated necklaces and bracelets, allergy bands, ear rings and many, many other items.

You could also have a mix of your home-made products and bought in products to increase your sales catalogue. It is entirely up to you.

Where do you sell the products from your new-found business? Here are a few ideas!

- Set up a counter display in a local shop
- Hold a house party 'invite friends'
- Attend craft fairs and local events
- Market stalls
- Amazon, E-Bay, google, ESTY and face book
- In your workplace

In addition to jewellery you could diversify and increase your lines (products) by adding accessories such as ladies' quality scarves, headsets, watches, purses and hand bags.

House parties are a popular way of selling your Jewellery. Your friends and neighbours will love getting together and will feel obligated to make purchases providing you make it a fun occasion.

As the host you can provide treats and savouries and a few bottles of wine to set the occasion. Human nature always prevails e.g. You will find that there are not many friends who will eat and drink at your expense without feeling the obligation to buy your products. Supposing you set a profit margin of 100% on every product you sell, and you invite ten of your friends. Each friend or customer spends £20/$20 10 x £20/$20=£200/$200 after subtracting the original purchasing price and manufacturing costs of £100/$100. Less food and wine

£20/$20 = your net profit for a couple of hours of fun would be £80. However, costume jewellery can often attract a higher profit sometimes + 500%.   How easy is that?

If you were to use all the sales outlets I have mentioned, then your profit would be greatly increased!

The house party and other methods of selling are not just confined to selling jewellery. This method of promoting and selling can be applied to almost anything i.e. Children's clothes, underwear kitchen gadgets, Christmas gifts and decorations, sex aids, car accessories and cosmetics and perfumes.

There is always a good response for house parties. It is an excellent way to socialise and make new friends. The retail parties can be arranged with work colleagues, neighbours, and collage friends.

Other outlets are local markets, car boot sales, craft fairs or from your own web site, E-bay, or ESTY.

Idea number five

My next idea is simple; it is proven and is so easy you will wonder why you never thought of it!

The next idea for 'making a few quid/bucks start with you! The first thing to do is to sort out your cupboards and wardrobes. Dig out those unused clothes, the clothes that have been in storage for months. They are clothes that you will probably never wear. Your clothes, your children's clothes, your partners clothes etc. Everyone has them! They are clothes you won't throw away, clothes you hope to get back into and clothes you bought and never exchanged. Some items have never been worn and are hanging in your wardrobe with the labels and price tags still attached.

The next thing to do is to launder them if needed i.e. wash and press them to restore them to their new looking condition. The clothes you choose must not be soiled or tatty. They must be in pristine condition. This will set your standards and will reflect your reputation and create repeat business.

The object is to sell as new re-conditioned clothes you would otherwise have given away or thrown away. The important thing here is presentation and determination to succeed. You must package your items in a sellable display. To do this you will need a website, an E-bay account, face book or ESTY.

When you have sorted your items for re-sale, the next most important step is the presentation and packaging your garments. You must then take good photographs for uploading to your selling platform e.g. (E-Bay) it is recommended you package the items in polythene bags with hangers. Add your logo, calling card, ribbons and flowers help, to create a good image on line. Set your price and don't forget to allow for postage and packaging.

With children and baby cloths you can sell these in bundles and make a nice display of several items of clothing in a fanned out display to create your photographs. Give a good description of each item and make sure you display the sizes. Remember to offer money back if not satisfied on return of the items. Make sure your prices are reasonable and affordable, don't be greedy. Remember you are aiming to building a reputation so that customers will return if they are satisfied!

Now that you have emptied your wardrobe of all those clothes you no longer had a use for and have a nice little nest egg, it is time to move to the next stage.

Every city, town and village in the UK is made up of a variety of charity shops e.g. Red cross, Heart foundation, Salvation Army, Mind, Scope, Rspca, and hospice charities. These organisations are dependent on donations of unwanted items made by the public, unwanted clothes and household items. They then attach a price tag to the item and display them in their shops, with the object of making a re-sale, often making greater profits than the original retail price.

Very often the prices seem quite high, considering they are donated free. To enable you to make a profit you may need to do a little bit of haggling or purchase several job lots to persuade the staff to accept a fair price. If you return regularly and the staff get to know you, they will be happy to strike a bargain. Alternatively, you could offer family, friends and neighbours a price for their unwanted clothing. Your friends will be glad of the extra money to spend, that they otherwise wouldn't have had.

Other ways of acquiring good quality clothing for re-sale is to advertise in your local paper, post leaflets, or ask at the local schools if you can display a poster or hand out your calling cards.

It is not difficult to 'make a few quid/bucks' however you have got to put in some effort, give up some of your time and plan, research and market your goods.

An example: supposing you acquired twenty items of baby clothes for £10 = 50p each. Then package them and displayed them at £2.99 plus postage you could expect a net profit of over £40. Hand bags, shoes and accessories depending on the make and condition can fetch £10 plus per item. Assuming you are able to make just 5 transactions per week minimum, you would be making an excellent return for your efforts. Just a visit to the charity shop or a deal with friends and an hour or two sat in front of your laptop plus a visit to the post office could see your bank balance swelling.

A success story

I will share with you a story I picked up on recently. A young student who followed the very same principle I have just described started out by selling her old unwanted garments on e-bay. She then asked family and friends for donations of unwanted clothing. She has been very successful indeed. So much so that she has paid off her student loan, bought a new car and put a deposit on a house. This is a brilliant and a very commendable success story.

So, what are you waiting for?

Find some paper and write down a plan and check list.

- Sort my wardrobe and cupboards out
- Start a Web site
- E-Bay account, ESTY, Google, Amazon, face book
- Print Leaflets
- Calling cards
- Visit and browse charity shops
- Mention to friends you buy unwanted items for a fair price

Good luck with your new venture and remember you must be determined to succeed! Don't give up! Believe in your idea and believe in yourself! If you don't follow this guide, then someone else will.

Idea number six

Gardening and landscaping is the next topic. Gardening can be very rewarding however it is both hard work and to some extent it is seasonal. However, there is work that can be carried out throughout the winter months. Example; preparing the soil, collecting fallen leaves, pruning shrubs, mending furniture and fences, setting out seedlings and greenhouse activities. Gardening can range from mowing a few lawns and tidying boarders to planning a major landscaping feature with patios, decking, ponds, and steps. Mowing lawns and tidying boarders does not require much skill and experience, however landscaping demands certain skills like bricklaying, flagging, plumbing and an artistic vision of what the finished project should look like.

Firstly, we will consider the simplest method of the two, mowing lawns and tidying boarders. This can be done in two ways. By using the customers own garden tools or providing your own tools. There are some draw backs to using the customers own tools.

(1) You have to arrange a time when you will carry out the work when the customer is on the premises or arrange access through trust.

(2) You will probably need access to water and an electricity supply so that you are able to use your customer's tools.

(3) If the tools don't work or you accidently break them, responsibility has to be determined.

The advantages are that you have no initial outlay for equipment and you only charge for your services at a reasonable hourly rate which may be £10-£15 per hour you could offer a discount for OAP's as a good will gesture. An average working day could easily produce a profit of £70-£100.

Advertising your new gardening venture can be done by leafleting or by putting an advert in the local shops at a very reasonable cost. You could also look at the neglected gardens in your district and have a chat with the owner to explain what your services are and handing them your calling card.

Landscaping is more complex and in most instances, requires you to have some form of transport. You also may need an account with the local building supplier to obtain your materials. You must also consider how and at what costs will be involved when disposing of rubble and waste materials. Landscaping will require estimations of time, materials, labour and hire charges which can be quite tricky. If you get it wrong, you can be out of pocket or even worse unable to finish a job. There is a way around this and that is to split each task into segments. This will enable you to estimate the cost of each stage of the landscaping job and have a prior arrangement with the customer to provide stage payments on completion of each stage.

The skills required for landscaping consist of, computer skills, bricklaying, flagging, joinery and many other job experiences. However, you may be able to sub contract the skills you don't possess such as Joinery and decking and bricklaying. It may be an added cost to employ skilled trade's people but if this guarantees quality and a satisfied customer then it is worth considering.

Garden produce

Tasks to consider are potting and preparation for the coming year. If you have access to a greenhouse then you should consider preparing seed trays and cuttings. These will provide you with an extra income. If you are able to acquire an allotment, then this can be another source of income. Allotments can be used to keep poultry and provide a source of income from free range egg production. Two dozen chickens will produce 140 eggs per week. The produce from your allotment such as vegetables will also produce a profit. Good quality produce can be sold door to door or to local shops.

Idea number seven

Advertising is going to be my next topic for 'making a few quid/bucks.' You may say, how can I make money from advertising? Well surprisingly, advertising comes in many forms. Advertising for any business or company doesn't come cheap. Advertising a product or a new brand is essential for businesses to get a product noticed. Therefore, to sell advertising space at a reasonable and competitive cost is a very respectable and profitable business venture.

The most common forms of advertising are:

- Television and Radio

- Newspapers and magazines

- Billboards

These are multi-million-pound advertising outlets throughout the UK and US. Advertising companies charge huge sums of money for their services. However, I am not going to talk about these large advertising conglomerates, I am going to show you a smaller and less costly way of entering the Advertising world and provide a great service to small businesses.

Setting up your advertising company cannot be done overnight. You will need a few skills and have the use of a computer. Also, you will require the assistance of a sign maker. The next skill you require is the ability to sell your method of advertising. You need to convince your client of the benefits of using your service and the ratio of potential customers noticing and viewing their advert (number of viewers or readers) secondly you need to persuade your client that if they don't take advantage of the advertising space on offer, then their competitors most certainly will!

The simplest method of advertising is to produce a small business guide using your computer and a printer. You could also design a calendar or a booklet. You then contact local businesses in your area and offer them a space on your calendar or booklet. Supposing you were to recruit thirty small businesses each paying you £5 per week = £20 per month for a monthly journal or business guide this would produce £600 per month gross profit.

The next method of advertising is using mobile advertising stand such as towing trailers with billboards. This can be more lucrative than renting out property. A billboard trailer containing an advertisement both sides can produce £140 per week or if positioned on a festival or country fair one billboard could produce £500 over a weekend. Other suggestions for siting advertisements are in partnership with farmers and land owners. This would be a profit sharing agreement in order to site your trailer in a prominent position, where it would catch the public eye.

For this method of providing advertising space you will obviously require transport and a few towing trailers. These can be bought new, used or if you have the fabrication skills they can be manufactured by the keen

DIY enthusiast. All the trailer making components can be purchased from 'Tow sure Ltd or motor vehicle scrap metal yard.' once you have acquired your basic trailers the next task is to assemble the billboards and fix them to the trailers. You are now ready to start selling your advertising space to local businesses; these can range from small independent traders to large corporate companies.

It is better to start your advertising by recruiting small businesses such as:

- Driving tuition instruction

- Double glazing suppliers

- Restaurants & caterers

- MOT, car repairs, and valeting

Make a list of small businesses in the area where you intend to site your trailers. Have a look around for pitches where you can site your advertising trailers, bearing in mind that you may require permission from the land owner. Your next task is to arrange a portfolio including contract papers, prices, discounts, and photos of your trailers and advertising displays.

Your next step is to contact a sign maker and arrange a price to have them make your p.v.c. banners with your clients' logo, description, what they are promoting and there contact location.

Finally, you are now ready to start selling your advertising space. This can be the most difficult task of all, if you are not a sales person or do not have the drive and determination. You need to be confident, professional and believe in your product. Don't forget you also need to be persuasive!

Using phrases like:

- If you miss this opportunity you will be missing a unique advertising medium.

- If you miss this opportunity your competitors are ready to advertise with us.

- Break the cost down into a daily charge £70 per week = only £10 per day.

- An introductory offer, the first three months for the price of two.

Visit your local library, buy books on line or visit 'you tube' to collect information on market research and sales techniques. Arm yourself with the knowledge to succeed in sales and advertising.

Once your client has given you the go ahead, it is time to meet your graphic designer (sign maker) Give him a rough idea of the proposed advertisements content, style, Photographs and the logos etc. and they will do the rest using the latest digital technology. All that remains now is to wait for your banner and attach it to your trailer hording and then position the trailer where it will be in the public eye with potential regular passing customers. Take pictures of the banner and give them to your client with a compliments thankyou note and a reminder when your invoice will be sent out including payment methods.

If you have followed this basic advertising business plan you are now on your way to receiving a good repeat income from your new business venture. Good luck!

The next area of setting up an advertising business is more up market, requires some investment and can be run from home, although visiting clients in person is more professional. I will introduce you to a basic version and a high-tech version, both ideal for those with computer skills and some graphic design knowledge; both are capable of producing a good return.

(1) The basic version of advertising idea is using board displays in public areas.

Example:

- Doctors surgeries
- Community centres
- Garage fore courts
- Dentists

With the basic version you will require several lockable display cabinets which can be purchased on line. The space around the perimeter of a cabinet is reserved for up to twenty of your own advertising clients and the centre section is used to display a map or aerial photo of the area, Public information, the opening times of the business, or a place for your client's customers to display private advertisements. The cabinet will be fixed in a prominent position on the advertising site. All your design work and graphics can be carried out and printed at home. Sales can be made by telephone, cold calling or by appointment. Sales techniques are similar to those used in the previous method of advertising i.e. the trailer hoardings idea. There are several ways to acquire areas to site your advertising displays, either by offering an agreed percentage of the advertising fees gained from the cabinet situated on their premises or simply offering a free space on a display you have sited at another location. A fee of £20 per month for advertising is cheaper than any media and twenty clients would produce £400 per month gross profit. Imagine if you were able to cover every town within the county where you live.

(2) The high-tech version of advertising is by using flat screen electronic display modules.

These can be utilised in the same way as the advertising display module/cabinet. However, the high-tech display module has the advantage of being able to use graphic animation and sounds. Similar to the advertising screens you see in department stores used to promote the latest household gadgets.

The purchase prices of the display screens units are around £100 each, including an integrated CD player or hard drive. Your client's business advertising feature can be a group of still pictures or an animated film. This can be achieved by using the Microsoft power point tool and arranging the client's advertisement on a CD, hard drive or a memory device. The display unit is then mounted on the wall of your chosen vender client's business premises.

Example:

- Fish and chip shops and take away venues.

- Doctors and dentist surgeries.

- Taxi ranks.

- Hair dressers and barber shops.

Using high tech video display units is the preferred method of starting up your advertising business. Using these displays modules has a modern feel to it and to be honest this is the future method of advertising. Using this version of advertising will also appeal more to your potential clients and will demand a higher value and increased profits.

The same techniques for selling advertising space apply. However, if you prefer, you could use a trained and experienced sales person to carry out the sales negotiations. If you lack the confidence to sell advertising space, that is fine. Hiring a sales person can be funded on a commission bases and their income depends on their results. You could also consider training a member of your family who may have a flare for selling, to carry out this task. You must bear in mind that you need your advertising clients as much as you can persuade them that they need you!

If you do decide to harness the help of a sales person, then this will allow you the time to carry on with designing and preparing your clients advertisements on your computer. It may be worth employing a young person with good computer skills for the role of putting together your power point CD's containing the advertising slots. Leaving you to visit the vendor client and fit the equipment on their premises. A timer can be fitted to ensure the advising is switched on at the appropriate times.

A good presentation on your video display module is essential to make your advertising business thrive, however like all the ideas in this book it all depends on you. You must have a plan, be professional, set your goals and be determined to succeed.

Idea number eight

Number eight in this book, 'Making a few quid' is entertainment. This ranges from busking, street entertainment, children's entertainment etc. This can be in the form of dressing up as a clown and learning the art of balloon sculpture or magic. Obviously, this type of entertainment is a speciality and it does not appeal to everyone. Working with children also has strict rules and you must be vetted by law. You must be approachable and patient friendly and pleasant.

Further methods of entertainment are listed below, however to do these you must possess certain skills in public entertainment.

<u>Examples:</u>

- Music and playing musical instruments

- Acting, dance & mime

- Escapology

- Singing

However, there are other ways of providing entertainment which do not require any skills. Entertainment can be provided at Galas, Carnivals, School fetes and car boot sales in various forms. There is usually a charge for your pitch, however, if you have plenty of bookings and there are a fair number of visitors on the day the rewards are quite good. The only overheads are your pitch rent and your liability insurance.

Examples:

- Raffles and tombola's

- Swing boats

- Bouncy castle

- Strike the bell

- Score a goal - Win a prize

- Pitch n putt

Idea Number Nine

There are many ways of making a few quid/bucks. Exploiting the sea and the beaches around the coast can become a nice little earner!

Example:

- Long lining

- Draw netting

- Cockle and mussel gathering

- Digging and collecting fishing bait

There is a demand for fishing bait such as lug worm, Rag worm, peeler crab, sand eels etc. These can be supplied to the local angling shops. Many fishermen cannot find the time to collect or dig their bait and can also be aged or disabled, and enjoy fishing as a hobby and pass time. They prefer to spend a few pounds at their local angling shop rather than finding it themselves.

Another example is to make and set your own fishing long line. Long- lining is the technique whereby a baited line of hooks are staked out at beach. Basically, the longline is a length of nylon fishing cord containing fishing hooks spaced out at intervals along its length, with the object of catching several fish on the incoming tide.

<u>Materials required:</u>

- Strong nylon fishing twine
- Traces made from 18lb – 25lb fishing line
- Standard fishing hooks
- Wooden or steel stakes(pegs)
- Bottle corks

The principle of making your long line is to lay your fishing twine out on a field, a quiet recreation area or your garden. Fasten your lighter line cut into fifteen-inch lengths at intervals of approximately eighteen-inches using a secure blood knot. The next step is to tie your fishing hooks to the end of the light fishing line using a blood knot and push the barbed ends of your hooks into the bottle corks for safety. The next step is to take the wooden or metal stakes (pegs) which should be approximately three feet in length and tie them to the to the each end of the longline.

Now you are ready to bait up and set your long line. The choice of fishing venue is down to local knowledge and the times and height of the tides. There is an element of luck involved and you must consider the dangers.

When the tide is fully out you will be able to walk out and set up your long line. It is handy to know or read up on fishing skills and what bait is popular or vary your baits. Flat fish such as flounder & plaice can be caught in a few feet of water and sea bass at the third breaker. Therefore, there is no need to journey very far out on the shore.

If there is a channel or gulley nearby it may be worth placing your long line near to this as this may be the main route the fish take when foraging for food. Once you are happy with your choice of where to set up your long line. You unravel it and drive the stakes into the sand until the hooks are lying on the sand.

You now have to bait up your hooks, the number of hooks can vary, some fishermen use fifty or more. When you have finished baiting your hooks it is advisable to time it so that the tide is now on the turn and heading back into shore. Bear in mind, you can sometimes be unfortunate and have your bait is robbed by sea birds or shell fish.

When you return and the tide is going back out, it is now time to see if you have been lucky this is also a good time to re-bait your hooks again ready for the next tide.

Long lining can be a hit and miss method of fishing however it is fun and can be done at very little cost. If you are lucky you can sell your fish door to door or use them to subsidise the family food bill.

Another fishing technique is to use a draw net. However, this requires some investment.

Example:

- Draw nets

- Use of a dingy/rowing boat

- A plunger

The method is to choose a channel or gulley at low water and travel along its length with the draw net adrift at the stern of your craft. By plunging the water as you travel the idea is to scare the fish into your net. This method is quite skilful and very hard work and of course to be successful the right venue is needed and knowledge of the area and tides.

When you can feel the drag on your net it is time to draw your net and get your catch on board. There are many draw backs and your nets can choke up with sea weed and debris.

There is another way of 'making a few quid' from the sea and that is collecting mussels is by raking cockles from the beaches and supplying restaurants with fresh sea food. If you are unsure how to do this then it is worth looking on you tube for advice and instruction.

Idea number ten

My next idea is a great hobby and craft which requires an eye for detail and the desire to gain and develop new skills. You will need a workshop, garage or shed, plus an assortment of Wood working tools.

If you decide to choose this method of 'making a few quid/bucks' it will be very self-satisfying, therapeutic and rewarding.

<u>Tools required to get you started are;</u>

- Work bench, vice and clamps
- A Dermal type electric tool with a variety of bits in several shapes and sizes
- A bow saw or similar
- Various power sanders and manual sanders
- Various knifes & crafting chisels
- Electrically heated branding iron/adapted soldering iron
- Branch loppers
- Hand rasps

You are going to source your materials from woodlands and forests and then you will learn how to transform these raw materials into:

- walking sticks
- walking staffs,
- shepherd's crooks
- Bows and arrows
- Catapults

When you have succeeded in making these products, you then have to market your very unique, hand crafted items. You can choose various outlets on line such as Amazon, E-bay, face book, google stores, and ESTY. All these methods of selling your product are good; however, there is no better way of selling than direct contact with your clients. By attending craft fairs, Agricultural shows, country fairs and many other venues you will increase your sales and enjoy getting out of your workshop from time to time. A good walking stick, staff or crook, crafted to perfection may take many hours and involve lots of skill and artistic flair. However, nothing is more satisfying than creating wood craft and having people admire your skills. It is even more satisfying when they are willing to purchase your product. A well detailed product can retail for as much as £100/$100 - £170/$170. Price is dependent on the detail and quality.

So, let's get started!

Firstly, you will have to locate a woodland area where you are able to forage for the raw materials you need for manufacturing your products. Young saplings, branches and off shoots are ideal, these can be crafted from willow, sycamore, birch, chestnut, blackthorn, hazel, Ash and other varieties of trees.

It does not take a great deal of skill to choose the perfect tree branch or sapling that you require to make a Bow, a walking stick or staff. Firstly, it is a good idea to seek permission to enter the woodland and cut your materials. Once you have permission to forage in the woodland, the time has come to scout around and select good straight branches. Once the raw materials are selected use your bow saw or loppers to cut them to the desired lengths.

Your skills in selecting the desired raw materials for your potential products will develop as time progresses and in time, you will begin to gain more experience. Of course, there are lots of tutorials on you tube which can be watched and this is a good place to acquire your inspiration. You tube offers tutorials i.e. From "Woodland sticks" and "The men in sheds" to the very experienced and intricate "Stinnet Sticks" which take you through choosing your wood to carving and decorating walking sticks with animals, snakes and birds,

There are many suppliers on the internet where you can obtain ferrules, badges, animal horns, stops, resin, seasoned shanks and many other quirky, decorative and interesting accessories used in the manufacture of walking sticks, and Staffs. Accessories for crafting hand catapults, and bows and arrows are also available through the internet search engines. There are also many books on the subject of wood crafting which you are able to purchase from amazon.

Here is a brief list of suppliers where you can purchase carving tools, collars, ferrules, embedded resin emblems, coins, and compasses, fishing fly prepared animal birds head stocks. Suppliers will also be able to provide books and video tutorials.

UK Suppliers of walking and hiking stick accessories:

- www.the stick man.co.uk

- www.The stick supplier.co.uk

- www.prestige walking sticks.co.uk

- www.Turners-retreat.co.uk

Staffs and hiking sticks follow the same principles as manufacturing a walking stick. From plain ordinary shanks to more elaborate designed shanks. To make catapults it is a matter of sourcing a good fork in a tree and cutting it down. Purchasing such things as 3/8"-1/4" elasticated rubber and acquiring strong wire twine such as solid 1.0 mm welding wire, or salvaged copper electric motor winding material. Make a cut in the forks of your catapult and insert equal 16inch lengths of rubber through the slots about 1.5 inches and fold around to the remaining rubber. By using your steel or copper wire and a pair of pliers wind the wire around the slots holding the rubber and wind wire around where the surplus rubber meets the remaining rubber. This should be pulled tight using pliers. Now take a piece of leather approximately three inches by two inches pierce a hole in each side and thread the remaining rubber strips through the holes and back on its self in the same manner as the fork slits. Once this has been achieved,

Take another piece of wire and secure the rubber strips on one side of the piece of leather tightly together and then repeat this on the remaining rubber strip. You should now have a hand-crafted catapult.

When you set your stall out at craft and country fairs, these items can be displayed as an added pocket money seller. Parents will buy these as a nostalgic item for children to show what they did when they were young.

They can also be used by fishermen when firing ground bait into a pond or river.

If you wish to expand your business and develop your skills further, you could diversify into other lines of woodcraft.

Example:

- ornaments
- Wall plaques
- Kitchen cutting boards
- Wooden spoons
- Key rings
- garden furniture

The list of interesting and useful items that can be crafted from wood available free from forests and woodland is endless. So, if you decide to follow this route to 'making a few quid' it is very rewarding in both income and therapeutic relaxation. I wish you Good luck in your new venture!

Idea number eleven

Most of us have visited the local supermarket, garage fore court, local shop or outside event and bought a sandwich or baguette. The prices can range from £1.60/$1.60 to £4.00/$4.00.

If you are like me, you have priced a loaf of bread and the ingredients used to make a sandwich and questioned the prices on display. For instance, a good quality loaf of bread would cost in the region of £1.60/$1.60 divide this by the number of slices = est. 16 slices = 8 double slices 2 sandwich pack, spread i.e. butter/margarine 5p/5c per slice. Total cost 30p/30c per pack. Now add the cost of the fillings i.e. ham, egg mayonnaise, corned beef, tuna mayonnaise or cheese which can be sourced for as little as 25p/25c per portion. Estimated packaging costs 20p/20c.

Therefore, the total cost of a double sandwich can be produced for less than £1/$1. If the bread and ingredients are purchased in bulk or from a cut-price supermarket the cost would be as low as £60p per pack, producing a potential profit of at least £1/$1 per sandwich pack.

The potential to make good profits from catering is out there. However, you must conform to certain hygiene conditions laid down by your local environmental health department and you must do your homework. It is important to do your research and decide where your potential market is and have an idea of the demand for your sandwiches and beverages.

Making sandwiches is only one area of the vast catering supply industry. There is also the outside catering industry which is huge and there is always a nitch in the market you can fill. However, some areas of catering require more initial investment than others.

Examples of outside catering:

- Roadside catering
- Events catering
- Car boot sales
- Industrial sites catering

What can you sell?

- Breakfast buns/burgers/Tea/coffee/soft drinks
- Sweets /toffee apples/candy floss/ Ice cream
- Fish & chips
- Donuts/waffles & crapes
- Continental food

There are many success stories in outside catering however the competition is tough, and many events may already be taken. You have got to be patient, research how to tender and at what cost your pitch will be. Many events are seasonal, and the weather can determine if your sales are high or low!

Many newcomers to the outside catering industry do not stay with it and give up after a few years and this is down to the individual not being suited to this business and the hard work and long hours required making it a success!

The most common reason for failing is probably their family commitments. Working in the outside catering business can be very rewarding, however if you have a young family you may be required to work through holiday periods and days when the weather is good, and families are out enjoying life while you are working.

Before deciding to venture into outside catering you need to plan your investment, decide on your venue and how many hours and days of the week you are prepared to commit yourself and your family too.

It may suit some individuals to provide a good roadside catering business with a lower volume of clientele, thus working fewer hours and producing a lower turnover. For those wanting a fast turnover and who are able sacrifice their spare time and don't mind traveling, working shows and events may be for you.

PRESERVES

Another catering idea is to make and supply homemade jams, chutney, sauces, and savouries. This is for those with limited time who would like to work from home whilst bringing up a family.

Your preserves will require good packaging, labelling and presentation. The idea is to spend two thirds of your spare time sourcing your fruit and ingredients and producing your preserves and one third of your spare time selling your products. Containers and jars can be bought on line and your fruit can be from natural resources growing wild in your garden, or bought from a wholesaler or grower.

Examples:

- Chutney

- Jams

- Marmalades

  Search for outlets for your product!

The secret is how you package and promote your products, for instance whilst visiting an outside market or craft event you will notice some stalls are more inviting than others. The reason for this is that some traders make the effort to promote and display their products in an interesting traditional way. Cover your stall in artificial grass. This will give it the outdoor countrified look. Use a nice printed open box with your preferred logo and position your preserves bedded in artificial straw at an angle, facing your customers. If you're selling jam or marmalade use a few whole oranges and strawberries in your display. Describe your products with positive words i.e. Delicious, mouth-watering, fresh produce, finest ingredients, the finest home-grown fruit, and made from handed down family recipes.

Another way of promoting your preserves is to source some weaved baskets to be used as hampers. The baskets can be found in charity shops and bargain shops or alternatively they can be sourced on line. Dress the basket with a nice checked or flowery material and line it with a bed of artificial straw. The next task is to make up a hamper using a selection of your jars of preserves. Add some fresh fruit and flowers to the interior of the basket and cover with some cellophane and ribbon to make a nicely displayed hamper. Attach your business display card or logo to the basket and you are now ready to sell new promotion.

Your hampers can be sold from market stalls, shops, craft fairs and many other outlets like garden centres. They also make useful gifts at Christmas and other occasions or even as a thank you to a friend or relative.

<u>Example:</u>

- Craft fairs

- Markets

- Speciality shops
- Basket Hampers
- Farm shops
- Garden centres

Idea number twelve

An interesting craft, pastime and lucrative hobby which many people turn into a business are leather crafting. This business will require investment in tools and raw materials. There are many products which can be produced with the right tools and creativity. However, the level of skills required can be very demanding. That is not to say the skills cannot be acquired. There are many books, videos and tutorials available from suppliers and of course there are many leather crafters who are willing to share their skills and ideas on you tube.

Example:

- Trouser belts & Tool belts
- Guitar straps
- Livery items
- Dog leads and collars
- Bags and wallets
- Wrist bands

To start with, I would advise you to visit several internet material suppliers' sites and purchase some books and tutorials on the subject. Alternatively, you can visit 'you tube' where there are many tutorials and people who offer advice and some of them have their own web site and blog spot.

You will need a spare room or home workshop with good ventilation and a work area. Start with simple projects such as key fobs. Purchase tools and material you need or improvise by making your own tools. Once you have mastered the beginner's skills and practiced the techniques you can move onto more intricate items.

Here are a few good tutorials you can access on you tube!

- Fischer workshops

- Weaver leather craft supply

- Back owl outdoors

- Leather craft academy

- Mall Brooks

- www.makesupply-leather.com

It is a good idea to use the winter months to build up your stock if you are preparing to retail your leather craft at shows and events. However, if you are planning to sell your leather craft using mail order such as Amazon, e-bay, ESTY, face book. Or if you are considering becoming a wholesale supplier and supplying outlets such as pet shops, garden centres markets etc. You will spend many hours crafting to keep up with supply and demand.

Starting your hand made leather craft business can be lucrative and rewarding, both financially and therapeutically. You will enjoy producing useful quality merchandise which will be admired by many customers.

Idea number thirteen

Our next idea of 'making a few quid,' Is for those of you who possess good computer and academic skills. Did you know that there are potential clients out there who are looking for skilled graphic designers, proof readers and CV writers, poster and leaflet designing?

If you have the required skills you could be earning a good income!

This can be undertaken at home and is a service with very little outlay. It is particularly suited to students and disabled people where every aspect of this venture is carried out in the comfort of your own home. All contact with your clients is within the frame work of the internet and your clientele can be world-wide.

Example

- Poster design & leaflet
- Proof reading, Essay's & book manuscripts
- Formatting manuscripts
- Book cover design
- CV's and cover letters

A good place to start with this venture is 'Fiverr' this is an internet sales and promotion platform site which allows potential clients to view their 'Fiverr' web site, view the services you have on offer and look at your achievements.

Once you have registered with 'Fiverr' your clients will be able to view your services and workmanship worldwide. They could be based in any country throughout the world and will contact you to discuss their project and agree a timescale and price. This is all done via the internet and payment for your service from your satisfied clients is transacted through 'Fiverr' who deduct a fee for their service.

'Fiverr' is a great way to launch your business services and is a trusted organisation. You will receive acknowledgements from your clients and these will be displayed in client's response area of your 'Fiverr' web site. Services start at a fiver upwards by agreement. As your 'Fiverr' business grows your ratings and level will increase.

'Fiverr' is an internet marketing tool and is not just confined to the subjects I have mentioned in this chapter i.e. graphic design and proof reading. 'Fiverr' can be used to promote many ideas mentioned in this book.

Example:

- Artwork/sculpture
- Photographs
- 'T' shirts and promotional items
- Collectables
- Business plans and presentations

I would suggest browsing 'Fiverr' as this promotional internet site will give you an understanding of how it works. You can view all the categories, items and services that you can use.

Idea number fourteen

Woodworking is my next topic and is for the DIY person and anyone with a few woodworking skills. Access to woodland and forestry areas is essential for foraging timber. The products you are going to explore in this chapter are as follows:

- Wild bird feeders and nesting boxes

- Rabbit hutches

- Dog kennels

- Bird tables

- Rustic country furniture

Once you have found a good source of timber, branches and logs you will require an open work space and a shed or work shop. The next task is to acquire your tools, these can be new or used.

It is a good idea to visit several garden centres and pet shops with your mobile at hand to take photographs. These will come in handy when you design your products and they will also display the retail price which you can use to set your own price. A good tip is to see what is out there and then improve the design to make your product more appealing to your customers.

Improving the design and appeal will also give you the edge if you are planning on being a wholesaler supplying the retail outlets.

Explore ways of dismantling or folding rustic furniture for transporting and storage. Make your furniture appealing, comfortable and adjustable.

Rabbit hutches and dog kennels etc. Try to design them so that they are easily accessible for cleaning and weather friendly. Don't use flimsy material and catches. It is important to make your products stand out from the rest. Quality is the most important selling point. The places to sell your products are events & shows.

Example:

- Agricultural and country shows
- Car boot sales & markets
- Amazon, E-bay, ESTY, face book, Fiverr.
- Pet supplies shops
- Garden centres/ garage forecourts

Alternatively, you could concentrate on becoming a wholesale supplier by setting up a wholesale website or approach the many retail outlets in your geographical area.

Idea number fifteen

My next idea is for the outdoor adventurous person. If you enjoy walking, then this idea may be for you. This very unusual pass time, hobby/ business are in demand, proven and worthwhile. You will probably not be able to make a fortune. However, you can 'make a few quid' if you are not squeamish and don't mind dealing with dead animals.

This next method of 'making a few quid' (Bucks) probably comes under the title of 'pest control' The British farmer is overrun with vermin such as rats, moles, weasels, and crows. The vermin spreads disease kills livestock and damages machinery.

 For example during the lambing season crows and magpies attack newly born lambs and pregnant sheep. This results in the loss of livestock to the farmer and reduces the numbers of expected flocks. Moles tunnel under the crops and pastures bringing stones to the surface which leads to damaged farm machinery which can be very expensive to repair or renew.

Farmers will usually pay a reasonable premium to have vermin kept under control. The vermin cannot be eradicated completely; however, it can be kept under control and therefore keep damage to a minimum.

Depending on the size of the farm, charges can be made by the acre or by the hourly rate. It is not excessive to charge fifty to one hundred pounds a day or an average of seventy-five pounds and produce three hundred and fifty pounds for a few days' work.

Tools required are:

- Mole traps
- A small post spade

When entering the area where the traps are to be laid it will be easy to spot the activity of the moles. However, one thing you must bear in mind is that moles can detect your scent; therefore it is advisable to wear gloves.

Where you see the mounds of earth, by carefully moving the mound you will discover the direction of the run. The best method if you are able is to press the turf between one mound and another with your foot. The moles run usually travels between the mounds in a fairly straight line. When you have located the run, it is time to dig a small entry so that you can install and set your trap. Squeeze your trap to open the jaws and place the ring in position.

Place your trap in the run and add a couple of earth worms each side if available. Replace the turf carefully and put a marker on the trap so that you can find it when you return. Repeat the process in several areas and leave the traps for a day or two.

On your return, retrieve the traps and display the dead moles on a nearby fence. This indicates to the farmer that you are doing the job he is paying you for.

There are alternative ways of exterminating moles using gas or strychnine; however, there are risks of ground contamination using strychnine and causing death to other animals. Trapping is the cleanest and humane way to treat vermin such as moles.

Crows and magpies can be dealt with using a home-made crow trap by constructing a cage and placing a dead carcass inside. Entry to the cage is one way and the crow's entre the cage trap but cannot escape. The vermin can now be exterminated in a humane way.

As I mentioned earlier this is not for everybody. However, it must be done to protect farm animals and crops.

Other services which can be provided for farmers are: hedge laying and dry-stone walling. These two skills can be learned by attending country and outdoor events, exhibitions and tutorials.

Idea number sixteen

DIY/ Odd job Man. We have all had a go at DIY at home trying to save money on the cost of labour.

<u>Example:</u>

- Painting and decorating
- Tiling
- Concreting/drive laying
- Flooring
- Plastic fascia's & soffits

It is fine to carry out this work on your own home, however to carry out work for a friend, neighbour or the general public it is very important that you have the skills and competency to make a professional job. It is worthwhile asking for someone else's opinion of your workmanship standards.

If you are confident that you are able carry out DIY jobs and have the necessary skills required, then there is nothing to stop you offering your services to the general public.

Many large building firms won't consider small jobs and if they do, they are usually expensive, and VAT is added to the bill. It can become very frustrating for the public trying to find a trust worthy person to do those odd jobs at a reasonable cost.

This service requires some investment and the use of some form of transport. Many building products can be delivered as and when required. This can work fine, providing your client doesn't mind supporting you by collecting additional items if required.

 You can work on a labour only arrangement where the client supplies the materials required and you just charge for your time. This can be a very satisfactory arrangement as the client controls their own budget for materials and can work out your labour charges by multiplying the hours you work by the hourly rate. Therefore a 7-hour day and an hourly rate of £10/$10 would produce £70/$70 and over 5 days would result in £350/$350 per week.

There are many jobs the average DIY person is capable of doing and those who are confident can tackle more intricate and larger jobs.

There are many courses at local collages such as:

- Brick laying
- Plastering
- Roofing

You can also purchase books and videos or brows you tube for tutorials. It is all about having the competency to confidentially do the work required. Any work you are unsure about and are not confident with can be sub contracted to a qualified tradesman. For example, if you were unsure about fitting a bathroom then employ a plumber. You can then concentrate on the décor. Remember anything electrical or central heating is required to be carried out by certified by qualified person.

Do not take risks! Safety first!

Idea number seventeen

If you are the type of person who enjoys working from home and would like to experience making and experimenting with creative candles, soap and bath products or confectionary then this is for you. This can be worked around your family chores and looking after the children.

We will start with sweets, chocolates, cakes and savouries. If you have the flare for creating beautiful specialised treats, then you will enjoy this idea of 'making a few quid'

There are many books and tutorials which take you through the process of making confectionary. Making handmade chocolates and savouries is an enjoyable and rewarding pass time. You can start by making a few simple chocolates and try your recipes out on your family and friends. As you progress into making dark, white and milk variations of chocolate, you can then experiment with fillings.

Decoration and presentation is an important area to consider. If you can imagine yourself being the customer, the artistic design on the chocolate says as much about your product as the taste. Added ripples, swirls and sprinkles etc. are used to decorate your home-made chocolates so that they look appealing to the chocolate lover. Displaying your chocolates in coloured paper, gold paper cups, and cellophane wrap and ribbon is used to promote your products.

Your kitchen will require clean and clear work surfaces. Kitchen utensils, and the usual pots, pans and oven are essential. The next step is to purchase good quality moulds of various shapes.

Once you are happy with your chocolate recipe, and sampled the texture and taste, you are ready to produce your very own brand of specialist chocolates.

Making savouries and cupcakes are also a popular product which can be made in the home kitchen and can be boxed and sold at country fayres, markets and other venues.

An excellent way to sell your home-made luxury chocolates is through complimentary gift sales. Presentation is paramount to promote your products.

<u>Examples:</u>

- Wedding table guest complimentary gifts
- Birthday celebrations
- Engagement parties
- Accompaniment to various "thank you" gifts

The gifts can be boxed, or cellophane wrapped and finished with ribbon and other decorative items.

Bath bombs

The next product is produced by utilising kitchen work area to manufacture home-made soap, candles, bath oils and bathing products such as fragrant bath bombs. Bath bombs are fun to make, and the ingredients can be easily sourced from local grocery stores, supermarkets and heath stores. Alternatively, they can be purchased from Amazon.

Example:

- Baking soda
- Citric acid
- Epsom salts
- Olive or coconut oil
- Food colouring (Optional)
- Moulds

Instructions and tutorials are available on you tube or by purchasing books on the subject through Amazon. Your products will look professional and all that remains is to present them in a well packaged and attractive way. They can be sold individually or if you prefer, a boxed display can be made containing home-made bath bombs, home-made bath oils, home-made soap, with sponge and flannel. This makes an excellent gift and can be retailed at house parties, the work place, car boot sales, Amazon, E-bay, ESTY and craft fairs and face book

The oils contained in your soap; bath bombs keep your skin soft and supple. There are many shaped moulds available and even fun moulds for producing kid's bath products.

Scented Oils

Another great product to consider is home-made bath/shower oils, shower gel, and massage oil. Recipes, tutorials and books are available on the internet and you tube. Books and supplies can be sourced through e-bay, Amazon and craft suppliers on the internet.

Ingredients consist of:

- Grape seed oil

- Scented oils Lavender, Rose, Geranium Etc.

- Sweet almond oil

- Sun flower oil

- Lemon grass oil

- Jojoba oil

- Avocado oil

- Vanilla, cinnamon oil

Peppermint (creates tingle sensation) It is advised to present these products in small quantities using glass or plastic bottles (glass bottles are recommended) these are available on the internet. For excellent you tube tutorials and advice on making scented oils "The English aroma therapist" is a good place to start. It is recommended to design and print your labels and instructions and display them on your bottles and add a ribbon as a finishing touch.

Home-made Soap

The next idea to compliment your home-made bath bombs is home-made soap and once again you can access tutorials on 'you tube' and there are many books on the subject available from amazon. Home-made soap, like other bathing compliments are fun to make and the ingredients are easily sourced from supermarkets and health food stores. If you prefer, you can purchase your raw materials from Amazon or other suppliers on the internet.

As soon as chemicals are mentioned many people shy away from soap making, as they see the word chemical as dangerous. However, the chemicals used in the manufacture of home-made soap are not dangerous providing you handle them correctly. Some of the chemicals and processes can be skin irritants and likened to caustic soda. As long as you take precautions such as wearing safety glasses, gloves, replace tops to prevent spillages and work in a well-ventilated room, you shouldn't have a problem.

The basic ingredients include:

- Sodium hydroxide

- Potassium hydroxide

- Essential Oils

- Fats

Like all the home-made products I have mentioned it is important to package and display your product in an appealing way. It is down to you to do some research and look for ways to promote and sell your products, however if you have the will and enthusiasm you will succeed.

Imagine running your own party plan and ten guests spend £20/$20 after manufacturing costs and a few bottles of wine and nibbles. You could find yourself making £100/$100 for a couple of hours work. Scented and ornamental candles have become fashionable in recent years. They are no longer the translucent white stick from the dark ages, used to provide light prior invention of the electric light bulb. The candle has now found its way back into the household as a product of many shapes and sizes which can be used to provide aroma's and fragrances around the house. Candles can be manufactured in your home and can be moulded into containers of tin, glass and foil. During manufacture the candle can be dipped in warm wax and sculptured into beautiful designs. Motifs, photos and special messages can be printed onto the surface of the candle.

Candle making has become a multi-million pound (dollar) world-wide business. These multi-million-pound (dollar) businesses didn't just spring up from know where. They once started as cottage industries or by someone trying a new hobby in their garden shed or garage. There are many books available on the subject of candle making on the internet, Amazon has a good selection and there are many tutorials on you tube to get you started. Like many of the home-made products I have mentioned there are several ways to promote and sell your products.

Example:

- Markets and car boot sales
- Craft fairs
- Supply shops
- Face book, Amazon, ESTY,
- Christmas & celebrations

Idea number eighteen

My next idea for 'making a few quid.' Looking after pets and dog exercising. Looking after pets requires someone who enjoys the company of animals, who is caring and devoted to their welfare.

There are pets which require looking after in the owner's home environment where they are used to their home surroundings. For example: birds, rabbits and exotic animals. Some people keep tropical fish and there is no way these can be moved when the owner is going on holiday or for a hospital stay.

These customers who require their pets to be cared for will require someone who is completely trustworthy and insured. Your service will be unique and will carry the responsibility of controlling and following the pet's dietary needs and securing the owners property. As an added security measure, you could offer to install a temporary c.c.t.v. linked to your mobile phone to provide twenty-four-hour surveillance.

The other pets you may consider caring for are Dogs and cats if you have a spare good sized out house or building adjacent to your home. Providing it is distanced away from neighbours property, so as not to annoy them! This would in effect be a boarding kennel or cattery. Of course, there are certain rules and regulations, insurance requirements and vet on call that need to be considered.

This can be a small venture and lead you into greater expectations depending on demand. The average charge at the time of writing this book for boarding a cat is £8-£10/$10-$15 per night. Therefore, if you are fully booked and have 10 enclosures you would gross UK £560-£700 per week and US $700-$1050 per week.

Next up is dog walking. Many dogs simply do not get the exercise they require. This can be due to owners having many commitments or demanding jobs. There are also those in the community who love a dog as a pet and enjoy its company, however they may be disabled or suffering the effects of old age. Through no fault of their own they don't have the capacity to exercise their much-loved pet.

That is where you come in! By becoming a supporter of your community and offering dog exercising. Collecting your client's dog by arrangement and giving it walking exercise and play.

Start by leafleting your local area, wear a luminous jacket or vest with community dog walker advertised with your contact number printed on it. You are now advertising your business free of charge. If you have ten clients and are able to exercise five dogs in a morning and five in the afternoon and charge eight pound per hour, that is £80/$80 for a day's walk and £320/$320 per month.

Idea number nineteen

Next a up is collection of Idea for 'making a few quid/bucks' They require skills and artistic ability or the willingness to learn new skills. They also require a certain amount of investment.

Example:

- Picture framing
- Lead/stained glass art
- Artistic painting
- Resin Art & abstract art
- Garden moulds/ornaments/sculptures

Picture framing

These can be stand-alone ideas, by concentrating your efforts, by focusing on one item, such as 'Picture framing for art. We will begin with picture framing. This is a highly skilled craft which requires precision mitre cuts and accurate measurements. The finished frame must meet a very high standard and when inserting photographs and pictures great care must be taken to get it right.

You will require a workshop or good-sized shed, woodworking machinery and tools. Your clients will be local artists, photographers and the general public. You will also require a selection of mouldings and other backing material.

There are plenty of books and videos on the subject and tutorials and suppliers can be sourced on you tube.

Art work

Some people are natural artists and have a born ability to produce life like images of landscapes, seascapes and portraits. However, there are many forms of art, abstract art being a popular form of art used to decorate the home, hotels and offices. You can take up art by joining a local art club or taking a few lessons at a local collage. This will provide you with the basics i.e. what medium to use, how to mix colours, scrubbing, blending and prospective.

An excellent way of presenting your art is to experiment with resin coatings. When producing abstract art Resin coatings give a great finish which catches the attention of potential customers. Many additional features can be added to the resin depending on your theme. For example, if you were to paint a night scene or space scene in a traditional way or even in the form of spray art and air brush. You could add sparkles, glitter, and many other unusual items from your outdoor natural environment such as grass, flowers bark, and seeds etc.

Using your imagination and experimenting with virtually anything around you can produce stunning art effects and may lead to you developing a unique style of your own. Art is an open book; there is no requirement to follow traditional art methods. However, it is advisable to follow art techniques.

There are many books, tutorials and videos out there and lots of artists willing to share their own experience with you. You will need a spare room or workshop with good ventilation, and light. You will also have to invest in some art materials. Such as paint, canvas or board, brushes, palate knives, sponges, and sprays.

Your art can take several hours of your time to produce; however, you can set your own price and sell your art on e-bay, ESTY, Amazon and face book. Art can provide you with a good return; however, it does take time, patience and the will to succeed.

Garden ornament moulds

The type of garden ornaments seen in garden centres around the country and on display in many gardens is the next idea for 'making a few quid' (Bucks)

Example:

- Bird feeders
- Animals

- Stepping stones/paving
- Edging

As a basic requirement you will require a workshop & open area/ storage area, various moulds, mixer, sand, cement, additives, aggregates, colouring, PVA, and a vibrating table, buckets and tools.

Practice makes perfect, so you will need to experiment to achieve the quality required. There are several potential outlets such as: supplying garden centres, garage forecourts, Markets and car boot sales. It is advisable to tour the garden centres and take photographs of the sort of products they sell and to take note of the retail price. Examine the quality and how they are displayed. There are many videos and tutorials available and if you don't mind hard dirty work you will soon be making a reasonable part time income.

Idea number twenty

The next great way of 'making a few quid.' (Bucks) 'Man with a van.' This idea is probably self-explanatory. The idea will appeal to those who have a driving licence or have the services of someone with a driving licence and don't mind some heavy lifting. There is a demand for 'pick-up and delivery' of goods from householders, businesses, DIY and charity shops.

All you require is a medium sized van and insurance liability cover and you are all set. Deliver your mail shots door to door, advertise using your sign written van and advertise in your local paper.

Business may be slow at first, however over time you will build up a regular clientele offering repeat business. Over time your services will become established. Offering house clearance and small removals can help your diversification into other service areas.

When deciding the charges for the services you are providing you have to consider your overheads such as running costs of your van, insurance costs, hired help and time and mileage. Therefore, your hourly rates must reflect this cost to be able to run a viable business.

This business idea is not for everyone as it requires lots of heavy lifting and manual work.

Another way of complimenting this business is to hire self-drive vehicles and box trailers. Although this will require a financial investment to get started, the vans and box trailers can be self-hired to the public to carry out their own removals and the transporting of goods from 'A' to 'B'.

It is worthwhile considering both these options!

Idea number twenty-one

Your next venture to consider is promotional items and trophies. Have you ever thought about supplying printed 'T' shirts, plates, plaques and mugs? Trophies and shields engraved for local sports such as football, rugby, snooker and pool teams?

These services are always in popular demand; however, this requires careful marketing.

Example:

- Acquiring low rental premises
- Indoor market stall
- Shared retail outlet
- E-bay, face book,
- Club and team promotion
- Fiverr & ESTY

There is also the need to purchase a computer, software, engraving equipment and specialised printing machinery for promotional 'T' shirts and cups, mugs and glasses. There are many products already made which can be purchase from a wholesaler as an additional retail item and many accessories to compliment your business. Table mats and printed items of local landmarks and areas of interest. Souvenirs with a local interest or theme can be of interest to tourists and visitors.

Craft Fair

Have you ever given a thought to organising a 'Craft Fair' or a 'Car Boot/Table Top sale? Organising and running Craft fair or Car boot sale is one of the easiest ways to raise an extra income.

Firstly, it is a good idea to visit several Craft fairs! Then once you have taken a few photos of other venues, speak to the crafters and give them your flyer and card. If they are interested in attending your own Craft Fair, write down their contact details. Tell them you will contact them with the dates and booking terms.

All you need to get started is access to a reasonable sized building, preferably with some parking space. For example, a Village hall, church hall or a community centre.

Once you have arranged the hiring of the hall the next step is to plan your dates, send out flyers and message to your prospective crafters and record the bookings in your diary. Print your posters and locate them at several positions around the area such as shopping malls, notice boards and public areas one week prior to the craft fair being held. Place an advertisement in your local paper with location, time and date the craft fair will be held. It is up to you what you to negotiate the hiring fee for the venue. This can be a percentage of your fees or a pre-arranged rental for the use of the venue.

Presuming you were able to attract twenty crafters and charged £10/$10 per indoor table/pitch and charged two hundred visitors 50p/50c at the door as an entrance fee. You could easily gross £300/$300 less your room hire fee 10% and stationary. Your net income could be in excess of £200/$200 for just one day's trading. If you chose to run the craft fair over a weekend the second day could be offered at a discount to crafters as an incentive!

Car Boot Sale

Car boot sales are quite popular in the UK, and are similar to a garage sale. However, a car boot sale is where similar like-minded people travel to the same venue and sell their unwanted household items i.e. Old toys, clothes, tools, bikes etc. for a reasonable price. This is an excellent way of disposing of unwanted items rather than taking them to the local dump. However, the advantage is that the seller pockets the money.

Car boot sales are simple to arrange! Firstly, you will need to plan the size of car boot sale you wish to hold. This can be as small as a school play/recreation area, a lot, or a car park or as large as several acres.

When organising your car boot sale, you may have to liaise with local police to control traffic from visitors and allow room for parking vehicles.

A small venue such as a school yard which can hold up to thirty seller's cars would not create the traffic problems compared to a large industrial yard or several acre plots.

You could expect to make £5/$5 per seller's car and an average of £50/$50 for each caterer. Therefore, if we assume a gross income of £150/$150 from sellers, £100/$100 from caterers e.g. Ice cream, Burgers/Hot dogs, Do-nuts your gross profit will be in excess of £250/$250 and additional income if you charge a gate charge/entry fee.

In the UK small Car boot sales only run for around two hours. It is therefore possible to run a car boot sale at two venues in one day or over a weekend, doubling your income.

Larger venues will take more organisations, such as car parking and traffic control and collection and disposal of litter. That said the turnover from a large venue would be much greater.

A Success Story

Friends of mine organise and manage several car boot sales at various venues in the UK. One of these venues is an old RAF air field near three large caravan/ trailer parks. Half of the total area of the air field is used as a car park for visitors/buyers and the other half is used for car boot pitches. On average two hundred pitches are taken up by sellers at £6/$6 per car £10/$10 per van and eight caterers at £80/$80 for a full day's trading with several thousand visitors/buyers.

The terms of the lease agreement are 50% split of net profit with the land owner and the gross profit? One day's car boot sale trading by the organiser produces in excess of £2000/$2000 gross. This produces an income of over £1000/$1000 for the organiser.

Idea number twenty-three

I will finish off this book with a list of ideas to help inspire your imagination into thinking of ways of 'making a few quid'. (Bucks)

Scrap metal: All scrap metal has a value from a tin can to scrap gold items. There are many forms of scrap metal in this throwaway society and there is an ever-increasing demand for recycling. Therefore, it is worth considering collecting scrap and reselling it to a metal merchant. This is a great way to make money with very little or no investment or start-up costs. 'There is a well-known saying! 'Where there's muck there's money' and it is very true. None ferrous metals apart from gold and silver i.e. copper, aluminium, brass and lead are plentiful. Copper from old electric windings, copper boilers and piping are common and have a good re-sale value. Scrap metal can be sourced from scrap cars, washing machines, vacuum cleaners, etc.

Drain & Gutter cleaning:

Not a particularly pleasant job, but a necessary one, and one that most people shy away from. Until their drains and sewers become blocked, that is! The weight of the leaves in gutters can pull the joints apart and causes leaks or even worse they can cause the gutter to collapse. A few tools such as a hand-held garden hoe, tongues and gloves. Disinfectant and a pressure washer will come in very handy for providing a professional service. A ladder and bucket for cleaning gutters will also be required. You could charge £5/$5 per drain and £30/$30 for gutter cleaning. Jet washing & disinfect dirty garbage bins. Cleaning driveways, footpaths and conservatory roofs can also become a regular service you could offer to your clients…. How easy is that to make a few quid!

Tropical fish & coral

This idea I would class as a specialised hobby and business. It requires knowledge of how to breed and keep tropical fish and how to grow coral. There are many rare and sort after species of tropical fish. To get started you need to purchase books on the subject, visit some tropical fish suppliers, view their set up and ask for advice. The internet is a good source of information and there are tutorials on making and stocking your aquariums. There are many accessories such as aerators, heaters, lights and much more.

This is a worthwhile hobby that can grow into a great business. When you progress, you will be able to mail your fish by special courier and use special packaging made purposely for transporting fish to your clients by mail order.

Flower/mushroom growing

If you have the use of a greenhouse or you can obtain a large poly tunnel, have an allotment or garden. You may want to consider growing flowers such as chrysanthemums, dallier's, roses, or carnations. Flowers can bring a good profit to those who enjoy horticulture and have plenty of patience. There are certain skills and knowledge required to produce and maintain flowers. Cuttings of shrubs can also be taken, rooted/grafted and developed as part of your flower business.

Mushrooms are also a great product which can provide a complimentary addition to your allotment or garden. There are many ways to promote and sell your produce i.e. Local florists, garage forecourts, local shops and markets or roadside display.

Thank you for purchasing this book. I hope you have found it interesting and I hope I have inspired and motivated you into starting a new business, a new hobby or pass time, which leads you into a rewarding and successful venture.

As I have said in my introduction, this is not a money making con trick or a get rich quick scheme and the ideas may not make you an overnight fortune. The ideas I have suggested in this book are proven ways of 'making a few quid/bucks' and are written to inspire you. Have a good think about each idea! Test the market! Explore suppliers! Work out your profit!

It is down to you!   Only you can make it work!

Ask yourself:

- Can I do this?

- Do I have the skills?

- Can I succeed?

- Which idea suits me?

- Do I need training?

I wish everyone the very best of luck with their new venture and I sincerely hope you have the passion, drive and the confidence to make your chosen idea a success.

*Please consider all the health & safety aspects when using tools and chemicals mentioned in this book.

Printed in Great Britain
by Amazon

17243734R00063